ARTHUR RANSOME'S EAST ANGL.

To Revd Victor Steynor in memory of the days we spent exploring

ARTHUR RANSOME'S
EAST ANGLIA

A search for Coots, Swallows and Amazons

BY ROGER WARDALE

POPPYLAND
PUBLISHING

First published in 1988.
Second edition published in 2001 by
Poppyland Publishing, 4 Alfred Road,
Cromer NR27 9AN.

ISBN 0 946148 57 0

Designed and typeset in Goudy Old Style
(with Book Antiqua display) by
Watermark, Cromer NR27 9HL

Printed by Printing Services (Norwich)
Ltd

Front cover: The *Nancy Blackett* in
Chichester Harbour, 1999. *Inset (top):*
Wherry yacht 1997; *(bottom):* a Broads
white boat.
Frontispiece: Horning Lower Street,
1996. Jonnatt's boatshed occupied the
left foreground of the photograph.

Picture credits
All photos are the author's except for the
following:
Brotherton Collection: pages 6, 17, 21,
28 (bottom), 31, 46
J. Russell: pages 8, 16, 27, 28 (top), 29,
30 (top)
G. Southgate: pages 38, 43

THE ARTHUR RANSOME SOCIETY
The Arthur Ransome Society aims to
celebrate Ransome's life and to promote
his works. A variety of meetings and
activities are arranged by the six regional
groups. There are three annual publica-
tions and regional newsletters. For more
information, contact the Society: c/o
Abbot Hall Gallery, Kendal, Cumbria
LA9 5AL

Contents

Acknowledgements   7

Introduction   9

Arthur Ransome   13

The Swallows and Amazons books   18

In the wake of *Titmouse, Teasel* and *Death and Glory*   34

In the wake of *Goblin, Wizard* and *Firefly*   50

Bibliography   63

Explorers' camp on Swallow Island, 1937. Left to right: Michael, Jill and John Busk, George Russell and two cousins

Acknowledgements

Without the help of a number of people, this book would not have been completed, and I am very grateful to the following, all of whom may rightly claim to have a part in it.

The late Tony Colwell, my editor at Jonathan Cape, suggested that I put together a book about the East Anglian stories and their setting. Victor Steynor put me in touch with likely publishers and did some preliminary work on the changes which have taken place in Harwich and Felixstowe.

Arthur Ransome's literary executors have very kindly allowed me to use extracts and illustrations from the books.

Gillian Beevor (Busk) talked to me about the time that she and her family had spent at Pin Mill before World War 2 and of how she sailed with Arthur Ransome aboard *Nancy Blackett* and *Selina King*. Josephine Russell was similarly helpful when I visited her, and she also lent me several photographs taken at that time.

Hugh Brogan agreed to the *Coot Club* extract from *The Life of Arthur Ransome* being reprinted, and Christina Hardyment sent me some useful correspondence which had been sent by readers of her book *Arthur Ransome and Captain Flint's Trunk*.

George Southgate has been my link with Horning and the Broads, and his input and photographs have been invaluable.

The late Martin Lewis made many expeditions among the muddy creeks of Secret Water and he shared his experiences with me.

Ann Farr, when she was working in the Brotherton Collection at the University of Leeds, was always most helpful to those with serious enquiries, and she looked out the photographs which the Brotherton Collection have allowed me to reproduce.

I am also grateful to the following who each made a useful contribution: John Berry, Michael Rines, Joy Wotoon, Jim Searle of the Norfolk County Sailing Base, Neville Khambatta of the Horsted Centre, Richard Woodman; the late Sam King, Tony Ward and Ron Watts at Pin Mill, the Norfolk Naturalists Trust, the Norfolk County Library Service, the Great Yarmouth Port and Haven Commissioners, the Broads Authority and members of Horning Sailing Club.

The River Orwell as Arthur Ransome knew it in the 1930s

Introduction

The haunting sound of 'Shenandoah' played on the radio at tea time on several occasions during the war meant that 'Uncle Mac' was about to read another instalment of *The Big Six* to BBC Children's Hour listeners. That was my introduction to the books of Arthur Ransome, and *The Big Six* has remained my favourite.

The wartime paper shortage meant that copies were almost unobtainable and my mother paid regular visits to the public library to renew my current Ransome and occasionally, when one was available, to exchange it. Eventually all twelve volumes stood in my bookcase and were frequently read. As soon as it was possible to do so, we went for a holiday to the Lake District to see if the country of the books really existed. We saw enough that week to

suggest it did, so when we returned home I wrote to Arthur Ransome to ask him if the places were real and if they were, please would he tell me where I could find them. It was the sort of letter he must have received by the dozen from young admirers, but he courteously answered it:

The only way to keep a secret (your own and other people's) is NEVER to answer a question. But you seem good at guessing. All the places in the book are to be found but not arranged quite as in the ordnance maps. You seem to be just the reader for those books. I am glad you like them. With best wishes from Arthur Ransome.

I felt that there was a challenge in

the reply and I was determined to be equal to it. For more than 30 years I spent most of my holidays in the Lake District and part of each holiday was devoted to 'Ransome hunting'. I recorded each success with photographs, and eventually, with some help from others, I found all the sites and it occurred to me that it might be worth publishing. Encouraged by Christina Hardyment (who had just had *Arthur Ransome and Captain Flint's Trunk* published) and Tony Colwell of Jonathan Cape, Ransome's publisher, I went ahead, and found a publisher. In 1985 I met the five surviving people for whom *Swallows and Amazons* was written. My Lakeland quest was complete.

A couple of years after my first visit to the Lakes, we spent a week at

Wroxham in Norfolk. I was delighted to find that Ransome had not jumbled the Broadland topography, and I could enter the world of the Coot Club in reality and not, as in the Lake District, only by exercising the imagination. Horning Staithe was just as he had pictured it and overlooking the river was the dentist's window in Banham's boatshed. My collection of photographs now included the northern Broads.

I have spent a further half-dozen holidays in Norfolk and have seen it change more than the Lake District. I wonder if anyone visiting the area now for the first time feels they are in the world of the Coots? I hope so. Much that Ransome loved – the wild rivers and hiding places in the dykes, the herons and bitterns and fish – can be found, but it is best to visit the area out of the holiday season.

Apart from the 13 stories, four books have been important. Taqui Altounyan's *In Aleppo Once* tells of her childhood in Syria and how they found themselves in an early copy of *Swallows and Amazons* sent by their 'Uncle Arthur'. Ransome's autobiography reveals much of his early life and influences, but ends as it becomes clear, in the 1930s, that the Swallows books are going to be a success. Hugh Brogan's *Life of Arthur Ransome* explains how the stories are thinly disguised non-fiction, and Christina Hardyment visited many of the places

River Bure, 1957

On they went, past the vicarage with the waterhens and the black sheep on the lawns by the riverside.

THE BIG SIX

for *Arthur Ransome and Captain Flint's Trunk* and included extracts of unpublished writing.

During the spring of 1981 I managed to revisit almost all the sites mentioned. I was shown around Riverside Cottage (once part of Alma Cottage) at Pin Mill, visited King's Boatyard, sailed on the Harwich–Felixstowe ferry, and had tea with Jill Busk, a most civilised savage, while she told me how her family had explored Secret Water more than 50 years before.

The majority of the photographs which I have taken over a period of 30 years aim to show the places as they appeared at that time; or as nearly as possible. Other photographs provide a record of places which have changed. The photographs taken by Arthur and Evgenia Ransome are particularly valuable. Not only do they show how things were in their time, but they also allow us to eavesdrop, as it were, on their cruises.

Since this book was first published I have enjoyed two grand celebration dinners at the Butt and Oyster at

Pin Mill, 1990: the Butt and Oyster and Alma Cottage

Pin Mill. The first was to celebrate *Nancy Blackett*'s restoration by Michael Rines in 1990 and the second was held earlier this year to celebrate her 70th birthday. The Arthur Ransome Society, which we formed in 1991, has brought enthusiasts from all over the world to explore the world of the Coot Club and the savage Eels for themselves, and the Nancy Blackett Trust has not only ensured her survival but has given numerous Ransomites the thrill of sailing aboard the *Goblin*!

Roger Wardale
August 2001

11

Arthur Ransome

The Ransomes were an East Anglian Quaker family. Arthur Ransome traced his ancestors back as far as a miller who lived at North Walsham in the sixteenth century. His great-great-grandafther left the area and became a well known Manchester surgeon, but his brother remained in East Anglia to start the Ipswich firm of Ransome and Rapier.

Arthur Ransome was born in Leeds in 1884 where his father was Professor of History at the Yorkshire College, now the University of Leeds. Cyril Ransome may have spent the term lecturing, writing and attending political meetings, but he was a countryman at heart and he had a passion for the Lake District and country pursuits. Until his death, which occurred when Ransome was only 13, the family spent each long summer vacation on an isolated farm near the foot of Coniston Water in the Lake District. While the professor fished for pike or sea trout, his young family were free to explore a playground that Ransome described as 'Paradise'. They made friends with the Lake Country folk and joined in the rural activities like hay making. The children played in or on the lake and some days they picnicked on the island nearby. That island has become a place of pilgrimage for Ransome admirers, some of whom have crossed the world to realise a childhood ambition and land in Wild Cat Island's hidden harbour.

His father's death brought a temporary halt to young Arthur's Lake District holidays and left him with a guilty feeling of relief, for the two had never managed to hit it off. His father despaired at what he saw as his son's irresponsibility and his muffishness. Arthur, who loved and admired his father, had looked in vain for his approval. He was a sensitive and rather wilful small boy, in some ways like the Roger of his stories. After several bitterly unhappy years at prep school in Windermere, Arthur scraped into Rugby. It was not until he was at Rugby that the masters found out he was short-sighted. This unsuspected disability was soon corrected by spectacles, and Ransome began to find life at school bearable. He had been writing stories since he was eight and looked to take it up as a career. However, partly to satisfy his mother who wanted her eldest son to find a safe job, he left to read science at the Yorkshire College. His university career lasted just two terms, and he was still only 17 when his mother allowed him to go off to London to become errand-boy to the publishing company of Grant Richards.

Ransome had no intention of becoming a publisher and after six months he had joined the failing Unicorn Press so as to give himself more opportunity to write stories and articles for newspapers. He also found himself a job as a ghost-writer of sporting books, and the first book to appear under his own name had the unlikely title of *The ABC of Physical Culture* (1904) in which he warned against the dangers of mixed hockey! This was followed by such titles as *The Soul of the Streets, The Stone Lady* and *Highways and Byways in Fairyland*. In 1907 the largely autobiographical *Bohemia in London* appeared and was his first genuine success.

Ransome enjoyed his Bohemian life in the capital and managed to earn enough to take regular holidays in the Lake District where he was befriended by W. G. Collingwood, the Coniston artist, writer and historian, and his family. The Collingwoods gave Ransome just the sort of encouragement as a writer that he needed and had failed to find in his own family. The younger Collingwoods, Barbara, Dora and Robin, were close enough to his own age to be good companions and after a year or

Ransome camped in the Yewdale Valley by Low Yewdale Farm near Coniston in the Lake District at the age of 24 while he was studying gypsy lore.

so he had proposed to both the daughters and had been gently but firmly rejected. They remained friends for the rest of their lives.

After his rejection by the Collingwood girls, Ransome developed the unfortunate habit of proposing marriage to any number of real and imaginary girls. Eventually, in 1909, he fell under the spell of Ivy Walker, and they married shortly afterwards. Ransome almost immediately regretted it, for Ivy was given to wild fantasies and Arthur was determined to carve out a career as a man of letters and, as others realised, he was not ready for marriage. Around this time Ransome turned his attention to literary criticism and wrote books on Edgar Allan Poe and Oscar Wilde. The Wilde book landed him in court when Lord Alfred Douglas unsuccessfully sued for libel.

Their daughter Tabitha was born in 1910 and although Ransome loved the little girl, in 1913, after Ivy had refused to consider a divorce, he resolved to get away. Ransome had always been interested in fairy stories and he had enjoyed the Jamaican folk tales he had heard in London. He decided that Ivy would not be able to follow him to Russia where he could collect fairy stories to translate for English children to enjoy. The result was *Old Peter's Russian Tales,* which has been hugely successful and has remained in print ever since it was published in 1916. There are those among his readers who prefer it to his Swallows stories. In 1984 a second volume was published under the title of *The War of the Birds and the Beasts and Other Russian Tales.*

Ransome spent most of his time in Russia during the Great War as correspondent for the *Daily News* and then covered the Russian Revolution, becoming close to the Bolshevik leaders. He felt it was his mission to keep the peace between the Soviets and Britain and acted as a go-between for the Foreign Office and the Bolsheviks, who recognised his unique position and took advantage of it. He claimed to have played chess with Lenin, and from time to time his duties brought him into contact with Trotsky's secretary, who issued regular bulletins from his office. She was Evgenia Petrovna Shelepina and they soon fell in love. Evgenia was a large, loyal, warm-hearted and warm-tempered lady who was to become Ransome's constant companion and severest critic. Eventually it became necessary to leave Russia, and in 1920 they were in Reval in Estonia enjoying a little sailing. Evgenia would almost certainly have been refused entry to Britain, and as Ivy still refused to divorce him, they decided to remain in eastern Europe.

In 1922 he had the ketch *Racundra* built in Riga in the Baltic, and the story of their first voyage has become a classic of its kind. At last in 1924 Ivy agreed to a divorce, and he was free to marry and return to England. The Ransomes hurried back and were soon settled in a tiny, remote cottage near Windermere. In order to buy the property they had, with much regret, to sell *Racundra* which was bought by Adlard Coles, the yachting writer. The cottage offered good opportunities for sailing and fishing and the

Manchester Guardian kept Ransome busy writing a weekly column of essays, and sometimes sending him on trips abroad. He was never fully reconciled to journalism and the turning point in his life came in 1928. Dora Collingwood had married Ernest Altounyan, another of Ransome's friends, and they returned from Syria for the summer with their young family. This gave Ransome the inspiration to write Swallows and Amazons, but he knew from bitter experience that he would never be able to combine story-writing with journalism. Loyally supported by Evgenia, he resigned from the Manchester Guardian and agreed in future to contribute only on a freelance basis.

The publication of Swallows and Amazons in 1930 proved to be a landmark in children's fiction and the book was quickly followed by four sequels. At this time Ransome weighed around 17 stone and looked very fit, but he was troubled by a duodenal ulcer and had other internal problems. It was

Arthur Ransome tying a fishing fly

partly because cruising always had a beneficial effect upon Ransome's health that in 1935 they began to look for a house in East Anglia. After some searching Evgenia settled on the Shotley peninsula and they rented Broke Farm, Levington, across the River Orwell from Pin Mill. Ransome quickly bought a seven-ton cutter he renamed *Nancy Blackett*. Neither of them had forgotten the days they had spent sailing *Racundra* and they vainly hoped to recapture them aboard their new boat.

They were quickly accepted into the sailing community based around Pin Mill, and cruising in *Nancy* brought him two books, but Evgenia thought the galley was too small and rarely sailed, so in 1938 Harry King, the Pin Mill boatbuilder, built him a larger boat. They called the new boat *Selina King* having commissioned a leading yacht designer, Fred Shepherd, who conceived a roomy cutter 35 feet overall, with a specially large writing table on which it was hoped Ransome would write more books. *Selina King* is a splendid yacht, and they

Arthur Ransome at the helm of **Nancy Blackett**

might have been able to recapture their Baltic cruising aboard the yacht, but the outbreak of World War II prevented them from having more than a few months sailing.

Just before war was declared they moved across the river to Harkness Hall near Pin Mill. Soon the Battle of Britain was taking place overhead, and the disturbed nights bothered Evgenia. They decided to return to the Lakes and bought a bungalow

beside Coniston Water. After a hazardous voyage up the coast to Lowestoft, *Selina King* was laid up for the duration of the war at Oulton Broad, and Ransome never sailed her again. Ransome, of course, welcomed a return to the Lakes and produced the final story with a Lake District setting, but Evgenia hated the damp climate, and as soon as the war was over the bungalow was sold and they were back house-hunting in Suffolk.

In this photograph by Arthur Ransome, Evgenia rests a hand lightly on the tiller of the **Nancy Blackett**. *The tiny pram dinghy towing astern they named the* **Queen Mary**.

This time they were not successful and for the remainder of their lives they moved houses between London and the Lakes. When Ransome was able to sail again, his doctor thought *Selina King* was too large for him to handle and he sold her. Laurent Giles designed a smaller boat which Ransome dubbed 'a sort of marine bath chair'. Giles called the design *Peter Duck,* but to Ransome she was 'plain PD'. *Peter Duck* is an eight-ton ketch and was built by Harry King in 1946. The design has proved very popular and since then almost forty yachts of the Peter Duck class have been built.

Finally, when he was 68, Ransome went to David Hillyard in Little-hampton and bought one of his five-ton sloops. He called the boat *Lottie Blossom,* after a favourite P. G. Wodehouse character, and she was kept in Chichester Harbour. They took her across the Channel and continued sailing long after Ransome's doctor had told him to stop.

The Swallows series was completed in 1947. The books had an enormous success in Britain and have been translated into twenty foreign languages, including Korean. Sales have reached well over two million in hardback and around five million copies in English alone. In 1937 *Pigeon Post* had received the first Carnegie Medal for the best children's book of the year, and in 1951 Ransome was made an honorary D Litt by the University of Leeds. He was greatly pleased by this and from that time he was always known as Dr Ransome. Finally, in 1953 he received the CBE.

The Ransomes' final home was yet another remote cottage in the Lakes, not far from the scene of his childhood holidays. Arthur died in 1967, and Evgenia followed him nine years later. They were buried in the nearby Rusland churchyard situated in a peaceful and rarely visited valley between Windermere and Coniston Water.

The Swallows and Amazons books

The story of *Swallows and Amazons* began with Arthur's holidays at Coniston as a child. The book also grew out of the happy summer of 1928 when Ernest Altounyan bought two 13-foot dinghies for his four eldest children to learn to sail during their eight-month stay at Coniston. When they had returned to Syria, and Ransome had begun to sail one of the boats, the *Swallow*, on Windermere, he began work on a story which was to remind them of their holiday in England. He built the story out of his own childhood holidays and put children with the Altounyan names into the story, with their boats and their 'Uncle Arthur' himself, thinly disguised as Captain Flint.

The Swallows or Walker children are partly Altounyans. The exception is John, the eldest. John is the steady and capable boy who would have pleased Ransome's own father and perhaps, looking back, Ransome would like to have been. Susan was named after Susie, but otherwise seems to have much more in common with Evgenia. Susie Altounyan was interned by the Germans when she was caught in France during the war, and made her home there. Titty, whose real name, Mavis, was never used in the stories or by family and friends, was the artistic and imaginative member of the family. She lived for a number of years just across the lake from the place where they learnt to sail. Roger Altounyan was a keen sailor and fisherman. After distinguished service as a pilot in the war, he qualified as a doctor and joined his father and grandfather in Syria where they ran a hospital in Aleppo. His later life was spent on research. An asthma sufferer himself, he developed the Intal treatment and the Spinhaler, which have given relief to millions of other sufferers throughout the world. Bridget was based on the youngest member of the family. Brigit was the moving spirit behind the formation of the Arthur Ransome Society and served as the society's first president until her death in 1999. As they grew up, each of the Altounyan children felt uncomfortable about their connection with the books. This was particularly true of Titty, who merely told her children that *Swallows and Amazons* was a story about some children who go camping on an island, and left it at that.

The Amazons, Nancy and Peggy Blackett, have no such easily identifiable originals. All Ransome said was that he remembered two girls playing beside the lake wearing red caps. The answer may lie with Taqui – the eldest of the Altounyan girls. Because there were too many girls in the family, Taqui was thought to have been turned into John. Perhaps the lively, adventurous Taqui was too interesting a child to have been left out of the story, so she was used a model for Nancy Blackett, the terror of the sea, instead? Ransome was always susceptible to tomboys, and in Nancy he created his ideal tomboy. There are other possibilities, including two girls who lived close to Coniston Water at the time the book was written – Georgie and Pauline Rawden Smith. Peggy, the most lightly drawn of the main characters, seems to have no original. There is one other possibility: the battalion of female soldiers serving during the Russian Revolution were known as Amazons. Ransome told his daughter that Evgenia carried a gun, so perhaps she and her sister were really the original Amazon pirates.

A sequel, *Swallowdale*, followed in 1931, but already Ransome had planned something altogether different. *Peter Duck*, the next book, is a swashbuckling tale in which the Swallows and Amazons are involved in a fantasy about desert islands, buried treasure and pirates. The story of the voyage to a Caribbean island was supposed to have been made up by the

children on board a wherry on the Broads during the winter holidays.

In her book *Arthur Ransome and Captain Flint's Trunk*, Christina Hardyment includes an extract from an early draft of *Peter Duck* entitled *Their Own Story*. The story switches between a beautifully observed picture of winter on the Broads and the fantasy voyage.

Ransome was right in abandoning his early version in favour of the published story, which some adults (but not the present writer) consider to be his finest achievement. The treasure-hunting voyage begins and ends at Lowestoft, and Ransome made a point of visiting the port to make sure of the accuracy of his portrait. He also visited Pin Mill where he had a dinghy built which he named after Peter Duck, and took out to Syria when he visited the Altounyans in 1932. Much of the story of *Peter Duck* was written during that visit. Ransome confessed in a letter to his mother that it felt a little queer after having lived with the children in *Swallows and Amazons* and *Swallowdale* to meet them once more as living beings running about. The old seaman after whom the book is named had appeared in *Racundra's First Cruise* as the Ancient Mariner. He was Carl Sehmel and he met the Ransomes when he looked after their dinghy on

The wild and lonely waters of Horsey Mere, 1999

a lake near Riga in Latvia, where he was harbourmaster. Sehmel had sailed in the *Thermopylae*, and, just as in the story Peter Duck asks to join the crew of the schooner *Wild Cat*, he had asked to sail aboard *Racundra* in order that he might go to sea once more before it was too late. Also in the story there is another interesting new character in Bill, the red-haired boy who claimed to have been born on the Dogger Bank. Ransome thought him rather a lark and a welcome change from the others. Most of all he enjoyed developing the characters of Captain Flint and Peter Duck and the contrast between the simple dignity of the former Cape Horn seaman and the impetuous, romantic Captain Flint is one of the joys of the book.

In the next book, *Winter Holiday,*

he was back in the Lake District with a story which looked back to his schooldays by Windermere when the lake froze over during the great frost of 1895. He looked back in another way too, for when he introduced two delightful characters he gave them some of his youthful characteristics. Dorothea is a literary romantic, and her younger brother Dick is a practical and resourceful scientist given to all-consuming enthusiasms. Ransome found them both very entertaining companions and, when talking with young friends, would introduce them into the conversation as if they existed.

Ransome had visited the Broads on a fishing trip during one of his spells in England when he was reporting on events in Russia: 'I had known the Broads in the far away past when, in an ancient wherry, I had gone fishing for pike there in the late autumn after all the pleasure craft of those days had been pulled out to winter in their sheds.' In 1931, Evgenia and he hired the yacht *Winsome* from Herbert Woods of Potter Heigham:

Our first boat on the Broads was one of the last two built by old Walter Woods of Potter Heigham. She was Una-rigged, with a gaff sail and the mast stepped close to her bows. She drew so little water that she could make her way up any ditch, and in her we explored thoroughly the Broads north of Yarmouth.

In 1933 they returned to the Broads, this time in a Fairway from Jack Powles of Wroxham. These were state-of-the-art sailing cruisers 24 feet long with berths for three in two cabins. The Ransomes had a regular programme:

Our favourite time for the Broads was immediately after the Easter holiday, when, in those days, the motor cruisers were for the most part lying unused and waiting for the summer. It was also the best time for birds. We could see the bearded tits, the big hawks over Hickling and Horsey, hear the booming of the bittern and some-times see one flying low over the reeds, and soon found that the birds have made up their minds that sailors are harmless. A rowing boat or a motor boat will frighten them from afar, but slipping silently by in a sailing boat or dinghy we were able to photograph great crested grebes on their nests and to watch, from only a few yards away, the parent birds swimming with their young on their backs.

During the first week of their cruise they visited every corner of the northern Broads and having arrived safely at Yarmouth at dead low water, they sailed through the bridges and up Breydon Water. During the next week they visited Oulton Broad, Beccles, Reedham and finally went up the River Yare to Norwich. Returning, they arrived at Yarmouth and the mouth of the Bure on a rising tide to spend a 'third week pottering among the easy waters of the north'. Ransome was always responsive to landscape and he was charmed by the slow-moving rivers and little dykes full of all sorts of hiding places. He had a notion of a plot for his next

Arthur Ransome sends the Jolly Roger aloft during their Broads cruise of 1938

The Death and Glory was on her way, water rippling under her bows, the tow-rope taut, chug-chug sounding from the Cachalot's engine, and the well-known banks of the home reach slipping by on either side.

Horning Reach, 1956

'Nobody's going to come waking us tonight,' said Bill.

It was as if in leaving Horning they were leaving their troubles behind.

THE BIG SIX

story with two priggish town children and a group of riverside children. Its title, 'Webfooted Grandmother', referred to a lively old lady, in marked contrast to Nancy and Peggy's Great Aunt. It was some time before he took up Evgenia's suggestion to replace the priggish ones with Dick and Dorothea.

It is clear from *Coot Club* that for Ransome the setting came first, the characters second, followed by some of the incidents, and finally he developed the plot. Once he had decided that the story could unfold through the eyes of Dick and Dorothea, his imagination raced ahead and the following April (1934) they went for a cruise to all the places in the story and Ransome took a set of photographs from which illustrations could be drawn, with the result that *Coot Club* is probably the best illustrated book in the series, full of charming tailpieces and accurate details.

The D's (Dick and Dorothea) meet Tom Dudgeon, the Horning doctor's son, on the train to Wroxham. They discover that bird watching and sailing occupy all his spare time. They meet him again later that day when Tom hides in the reeds beside the yacht they are using as a houseboat while they are staying with Mrs Barrable, their mother's former teacher. Mrs Barrable is the development of the webfooted grandmother idea. Tom has to hide because he is fleeing from a pursuing motor-cruiser full of Hullabaloos whom he has cast off because they were moored by a favourite coot's nest with eggs about to hatch, and it was the only thing he could do to save the chicks. The Hullabaloos had been told about the nesting coot by some other members of the Coot Club, the piratical Death and Glories, but had refused to move. Soon the newcomers have become acquainted with the locals and the *Teasel* becomes a training ship, as Tom's neighbours, Port and Starboard

Margoletta *look-alike, 1996*

'Dick,' she cried. 'It's them. The Margoletta. They've come back. No, don't look at them. Go on looking at the black sheep...'
With roaring engine and a tremendous blare of band music from the gramophone on the foredeck, the big cruiser passed them.

COOT CLUB

23

Rivals for **Flash**: *white boats taking part in Horning Regatta Week, 1972*

Farland, and the Death and Glories join forces to help Tom keep clear of the avenging Hullabaloos, and at the same time teach Dick and Dorothea how to sail. Tom is chased all over the Broads by the Hullabaloos, as the *Teasel* follows the Ransomes' cruise around the northern Broads and down to the southern waters. Eventually the Hullabaloos ram a beacon post on Breydon Water and are salved by the Death and Glories.

The setting of *Coot Club* is almost completely accurate. Unlike the Lake District stories where the elements of a real-life landscape are moved around and blended to make a life-like fictional one, Ransome accepted the constraints imposed by reality. Tom Dudgeon's house with its golden bream weather vane and waterside lawn is an exception and was not to be found in Horning reach, although there are several dykes and houses which would have made admirable homes for the Farland family. The three Death and Glories would not have been able to have established such an impeccable alibi as weeding in the neighbouring policeman's garden, because in the 1930s Horning was policed by the constable from Ludham. Mr Farland was clearly a member of Horning Sailing Club and he raced a White Boat – a 20-foot Yare and Bure One Design. Ransome went strangely adrift with the name *Flash,* as all the class members are named after butterflies or moths. Per-haps he thought that if he chose a butterfly there would be a clamour of new boat owners wanting to be the first to use the name.

I have tried in vain to find any reference to the 'Yarmouth Sharks' who, according to *Coot Club,* lured the unsuspecting visitor into allowing them aboard, and when they had run the yacht into trouble sailing through the bridges had to be rescued by their accomplices who claimed salvage. A couple of local historians failed also in their search, but one made the suggestion that such a thing could very well have happened in Victorian times.

Locally it is believed that *Teasel* was one of the sailing cruisers hired out by Percy Hunter's yard at Womack Dyke, Ludham, which are still sailing today. Perhaps *Teasel* was a four-berth variation of the Fairway. Some of the incidents in the story occurred to the Ransomes on that 1934 voyage around the Broads. The Ransomes also met an ice-cream seller at Potter Heigham, towed through Yarmouth, moored close to a Thames barge in

Beccles, saw a fisherman with an eel-bab and were towed back through Yarmouth by a tug remarkably like the *Come Along*. William, Mrs Barrable's pug, was owned by Margaret and Charles Renold who were fishing friends from Cheadle and who had taken a keen interest in the progress of the story.

Hugh Brogan, Ransome's biographer, says of *Coot Club*:

The result was a worthy successor to Winter Holiday. *If at times it touches greatness, it is for a reason barely to be glimpsed in Ransome's working notes. In the writing, the war between the bird-protector Tom and the motor-cruising Hullabaloos, with their gramophone, radio, yachting-caps and beach-pyjamas, became symbolic of the forces contesting the future of the Broads. The more Ransome detailed the society of the Bure, the Thurne and the Waveney the more clearly he showed that more was at stake than the future of a child-outlaw. The book gained greatly in force since Ransome scrupulously accepted the constraints of chronology and geography. The result was a wonderful picture of the Norfolk waters at a crucial moment of transition. The activities of the RSPB had brought back the bitterns, but the day of the wherry was almost over. The lorry, the radio (later, television), the motor-car, agrarian greed, government policy, sewage and artificial fertilisers were going to do more to undermine the social and natural life of the Broads than Ransome began to guess. In life, the Hullabaloos were going to win. That does not make their defeat in fiction less pleasing; it makes Ransome's scrupulous portrayal of the Broads in 1933 all the more valuable and interesting; and it reminds us that the issues he chose to write about were not trivial: especially not to him. As he had loved the old Russia and the traditional Lake District, so he loved the old Norfolk.* Coot Club *and certain passages of* The Big Six *are his vindication of that love.*

Nancy Blackett in Chichester Harbour, 1999

Pigeon Post, which followed in 1936, brought a return to the Lake country and is a land-based affair of gold mining in the fells. But before it was completed, the Ransomes had left the Lake District and had rented Broke Farm, near Ipswich, close to the River Orwell, and he was the proud owner of a 7-ton cutter, the *Nancy Blackett*. She has four berths and measures 28 feet overall with a beam of eight feet and was built

On the hard, men were walking round a barge that had been afloat in the middle of the day, and were busy with scrapers and tar-brushes.

WE DIDN'T MEAN TO GO TO SEA

by David Hillyard, the well-known Littlehampton builder of sturdy, seamanlike cruisers. Just as *Racundra* and *Swallow* had been translated into print, so *Nancy Blackett* was to provide the starting point for an exceptional story. Once more, the crew of his yacht were the Swallows. John was now ready to skipper something larger than poor *Swallow* which was sold when the Ransomes left the Lake District. Ransome relished the technical problems. With his customary thoroughness he took *Nancy* across to Holland in order to test the accuracy of his idea and gather some local

Barges on the hard at Pin Mill, 1972

colour. The voyage turned out to be rather more like the story than he expected, for the young man he took as crew turned out to be hopelessly inadequate and Ransome spent 20 hours at the helm before they made their landfall in Holland.

In the story the Swallows and their

mother arrive at Pin Mill to await the return of Commander Walker from a tour of duty abroad. They stay at Alma Cottage with Miss Powell. Here Ransome was strictly accurate for Annie Powell lived at Alma Cottage and let rooms. She did not have the reputation for making omelettes that he claimed for her, but after publication readers turned up and expected omelettes, so the poor woman had to set to and oblige. Soon after their arrival, the Swallows meet a young man, Jim Brading, sailing *Goblin* to her anchorage off Pin Mill. *Goblin* is, of course, *Nancy Blackett*, and portrayed with great affection and attention to detail. Jim Brading was probably modelled on Jim Clay, whose father wrote for the *Manchester Guardian*, and who was about to go up to Oxford when they first met in 1935. Jim invites the Swallows to crew for him for a couple of days until they are due to meet their father on his return from the Far East. They promise not to go outside the harbour. On the second morning, after sailing to the harbour mouth, a calm forces them to use the engine in order to keep their promises, but Jim had run the tank almost dry the previous day and they soon run out of petrol. The *Goblin* anchors on the Shelf opposite Harwich, and Jim rows ashore to Felixstowe for petrol. In his hurry he runs head-first into an Eastern Counties bus, and is whisked away to hospital, but the Swallows, still on board the *Goblin*, know nothing of this. A fog closes in and as the tide rises *Goblin* drags her anchor and drifts out to sea on the first of the ebb. The fog lifts, only to be replaced by heavy rain and strong offshore winds. There is nothing for it but to sail on. The following morning they signal for a pilot who takes them into Flushing where their father is just in time to make a pierhead jump from his steamer and, after a brief stay in Holland, he sails the *Goblin* back to England.

The heart of the book is the unsought voyage and the response of the children, particularly John and Susan, to real danger. Ransome tells the story in a simple, straightforward manner and succeeds in making the children's heroism believable, because at all times they respond and behave like children. Many people, including Ransome himself, I suspect, consider *We Didn't Mean to Go to Sea* (1937) his masterpiece. The story could very well have been inspired by Maurice Griffiths' account of a voyage to Holland aboard his wife's yacht in *The Magic of the Swatchways* published in 1932. The Griffiths drifted out of Harwich harbour in a fog. Mrs Griffiths was horribly sick, and there were several other similarities to the Swallows' epic crossing.

The Ransomes spent five happy years at Pin Mill. In the Lakes they had lived in isolation in remote cottages,

George Russell at the time that he began to sail with Arthur Ransome

Gillian and John Busk aboard
Lapwing, 1938

lovely unspoilt area of mud and ever-changing tides known as the Walton Backwaters. This became the setting of his next book, *Secret Water,* which was published in 1939, and which sprang from a few days spent there in company with *Lapwing,* the eight-ton cutter belonging to the Busk family.

They had met the family one day at Pin Mill when the children were noisily practising capsizing under the watchful eye of their father. Asking what all the commotion was about, Ransome was told, 'Oh, it's only the Busks'. This was just the sort of thing to appeal to the boyish side of

but on the East Coast Arthur had a number of local friends including several families of children who helped him with the winter work on *Nancy.*

Evgenia was not impressed by *Nancy Blackett* and thought the galley too small for the sort of cooking she liked to do aboard ship and so she rarely sailed. Help was at hand, however, in the form of two enthusiastic teenagers, George and Josephine Russell who lived next door at Broke Hall and could be relied upon to crew and to help with the winter chores and the fitting out whenever they were not at school. Ransome only made short passages with the children, and one of their favourite haunts was that

Lapwing *at Pin Mill, 1938*

Real-life map-makers, 1937: the Busk family sailing in Goblin Creek after a map-making expedition in Secret Water

Ransome's character. Very soon they had become friends. The Busks lived at The Grange, Chalmondiston, just along the road from Pin Mill. The children, John, Michael and Gillian, were enthusiastic readers of the Swallows books, and they had a dinghy called *Wizard,* whose name was borrowed for the story, and another dinghy, *Zip.*

Lapwing arrived at Hamford Water and her crew had a blank map like the one in *Secret Water* which had been drawn by Major Busk. They set out to complete the map with their own explorations – just as the Swallows do in the story. Each day the parents and Michael, the youngest, sailed *Wizard* and took the food; John and his cousin sailed *Zip,* and Jill and Major Busk's godson sailed *Jo,* a borrowed dinghy which was a poor sailer. After a morning of exploration they met at a prearranged spot for lunch, after which the exploration continued until the dinghies returned to base for the evening meal and the filling-in of the map with parts explored that day.

A day or so after the *Lapwing* arrived, *Nancy Blackett* appeared in Hamford Water with George and Josephine Russell as her crew and flying the Jolly Roger. The exploration party was now complete. Jill, now Mrs Gillian Beever, remembers that the setting was not completely accurate. Blackberry Coast to the north of Secret (Hamford) Water was covered at high water, and they did not discover the North-east or North-west

*Josephine Russell using two hands to hold the **Nancy Blackett** on course*

passages. The creek leading to Witch's Quay was rather easier to navigate than Nancy and the Swallows found it, and the little creek leading out of Amazon Creek was put in to provide a plausible excuse for Titty to delay her crossing of the Red Sea. The young Busks were put into the story as the mud-patterned tribe of savages, the Eels, Daisy, Dum and Dee. Eventually, when the book was published it was dedicated to the Busk family.

Some years later, shortly after the war, when Ransome was at Pin Mill with his cruiser *Peter Duck,* he was rather bothered by some young admirers and their questions. He looked across and saw Gillian, who was just out of naval uniform, and told the children, 'There's Daisy. You go and ask her'. As a general rule, Ransome was not keen on children and Evgenia became good at protecting him from too much attention. He remained partly a child, and Gillian remembers that tea was always taken backwards, starting with the most exciting cakes and finishing up with the bread and butter.

In the story the Swallows are marooned with a borrowed dinghy on the largest island and have to make a map of the area. They have the vaguest of blank maps and stern instructions not to go out to sea again. Soon they meet the Mastodon boy who lives in a derelict barge nearby and agrees to be their native guide. Unexpectedly the Amazons arrive, also with a borrowed dinghy, and with the news that the Mastodon is expecting the rest

Cooking and steering

of his savage tribe Nancy finds the thought of war much more stimulating than mere map making. By the time they have to leave the map is finished — just — and Nancy has her war, but there is plenty of tension and the introduction of Bridget, joining her elders for the first time, is a welcome relief. Bridget has no idea of the tension around her and is determined to enjoy every minute. In her straightforward, direct way she has the effect of unifying the cast of 13, and it is a great pity she was excluded from the remainder of the series.

During this time, up to the start of World War 2, the Ransomes continued to sail in Broads cruisers, often accompanied by young friends who had hired similar yachts. Mostly these came from their sailing friends at Pin Mill, but in 1938 they were joined by two of the Altounyans. Taqui and Titty sailed a tiny cruiser, the *Whippet,* and proved to be the most accomplished of the younger sailors. The Ransomes continued to sail Fairway yachts and once Ransome hired a motor cruiser with Charles and Margaret Renold in order to go fishing for pike. It was Margaret Renold who first suggested that he should write a detective story.

George Owdon, who had aided the Hullabaloos in *Coot Club,* was an ideal villain and, after first resolving that the story would not again involve visitors' boats, Ransome wrote his masterly thriller about the casting off of craft from Broadland staithes. *The Big Six* is set at the end of the summer holidays during which the Death and

Ransome towing the Fairway yacht under the Potter Heigham bridges, 1934

Glories have put a stove and cabin with bunks into their old boat. Ransome clearly had a particular boat in mind because I found a diagram in one of his notebooks which gives the length as 21 feet and the depth as 4 feet. This corresponds exactly with

the size of one of the boats in a list of regulation lifeboats. These additions to their old boat will ensure that the Coot Club will be able to keep a better watch over the birds the following spring. George Owdon, who is known to steal rare birds' eggs to increase his already ample pocket money, decides to discredit the Coot Club by casting off boats wherever the Death and Glories go. Naturally enough, everyone remembers Tom's affair of the spring and believes the Coots to be guilty. Only with the timely arrival of Dick and Dorothea do the Coot Club start some detective work of their own. The climax is as exciting and satisfying as anything that Ransome wrote.

In the course of the story there is more information about life in Broadland, and it presents a charming portrait of village life. There is a memorable incident when the Death and Glories catch a 30½ lb pike. This was probably inspired by the 21 lb pike which used to hang in the Swan Inn, having been caught by 12-year-old Edward Gillard in 1921, and is mentioned in the story. Another incident woven into the story is the visit to the eel man, George Parker, who had his sett near Black Horse Broad. He was not as venerable as Harry Bangate but was Horning eelman for 47 years until he retired just before World War 2. There are almost certainly no originals of Joe, Bill and Pete, who were introduced in *Coot Club* as interesting minor characters rather as Bill had been in *Peter Duck*. They are put firmly centre stage in *The Big Six* and it is clear Ransome felt considerable warmth for the three part-owners of the *Death and Glory*. He had given them full names: Joe Southgate, Bill Jenkins, Pete Woods, although these never appear in the stories. This is an example of how Ransome liked to know more about his characters than he put into the books.

The Roaring Donkey public house is not to be found, although exploring the upper reaches of the River Thurne some years ago, I discovered the dyke, just as described, but found that it ended in the middle of nowhere. A Roaring Donkey Inn can be found near Clacton and doubtless Ransome came across the name on one of his visits to the Walton Backwaters.

In *Missee Lee* (1941) Captain Flint and the Swallows and Amazons lose the *Wild Cat* by fire in the China Seas. They are captured by Chinese pirates and eventually escape aboard a Chinese junk. The chief delight of the story is the character of Missee Lee, the pirate chief who abandoned an academic career at Cambridge to return to take over the business from her dying father. The eleventh book in the series tells of the Amazons and D's in the Lake country, and the series closed with a tale involving the Swallows, Amazons and D's sailing aboard an old pilot cutter with Captain Flint, *Great Northern?* (1947). Dick spots a great northern diver nesting in Great Britain for the first time somewhere in the Outer Hebrides. A wealthy egg-collector has to be outwitted and the birds saved. Sadly the Coots are not involved.

For almost 40 years there were 12 stories in the series, but Ransome began at least one more. Nobody knew of the manuscript's significance until Hugh Brogan discovered the folder in a drawer of the Ransome Room at the Abbot Hall Museum in Kendal, where there is a fascinating collection of manuscripts, books,

Boatsheds at Horning

sketchbooks, flags and artefacts given by Evgenia.

Hugh Brogan has called the story *Coots in the North* and although only the first few chapters exist in what seems to be a first draft, since its publication readers have come to know Joe, Bill and Pete rather better. The story was not, as originally thought, Ransome's final fling with his Swallows and Amazons, for in one of his sketchbooks, preceding the sketches for his next published story, *Great Northern?*, I found seven drawings illustrating incidents in *Coots in the North*.

The story opens in August and the *Death and Glory* is moored outside Jonnatt's boatshed because the staithe is full of visitors' boats. The boys have nothing to do. At this time of the year the birds can look after themselves and when they help visitors in trouble they are lucky to get a 'thank you'. Tom and the twins are on holiday and the D's are in the Lakes. The Death and Glories watch a cruiser being loaded on a trailer for a long journey by Pete's father and other boatbuilders. She is being taken to the lake in the north where the D's are. Following a chance remark by Mrs Barrable, Joe decides that they will stow away. He neatly tricks Bill and Pete into hiding aboard, and off they go. When they arrive at the lake the boys make friends with the cruiser's owner and borrow a dinghy in order to look for the D's. Eventually they meet, but not before the Coots have fallen foul of Nancy Blackett.

The fascinating prospect of the tensions and contrasts between the Swallows and Amazons and the Death and Glories remains unfulfilled, although there are notes on how the story could develop and end. It is doubtful if we shall ever know for sure why it was abandoned, but there is no doubt of the quality of what there is. It is vintage Ransome.

In the wake of *Titmouse, Teasel* and *Death and Glory*

The Broads themselves are the remains of water-filled mediaeval pits made by digging for the peat that was used locally as fuel or taken to Norwich. When Ransome first sailed here, the water was sparkling clear, visitors were few and pleasure boats like rowing boats with awnings, converted wherries and slender sailing yachts shared the river with the trading wherries, which still had an important part to play in the local economy.

In *Coot Club,* the Norfolk and Suffolk Broads were in a period of transition. The increasing number of motor cruisers for hire was bringing a new kind of visitor while the wherries were becoming fewer each year. Today, due to an increase in phosphate from sewage and nitrate from adjacent farmland, the rivers are cloudy, the Broads are silting up. The algae which have flourished in the nutrient-rich layer have shaded the light from aquatic plants, which has in turn brought about decline in the variety of aquatic animals. Constant stirring-up of the rivers by motor cruisers has made things worse. The Broads Authority *Broads Plan* of 1987 outlined ways in which phosphate levels might be reduced, water quality improved and water plants re-established. The situation is improving. In 1981 Cockshoot Broad was cut off from the River Bure by a dam, and 40,000 cubic yards of mud were pumped out. The experiment has been a complete success and the results can be seen by visitors who can park opposite the Ferry Inn and follow the river bank to the dyke and then use the wooden walkway over the marshy ground to reach the broad.

To me the most abrasive change since Ransome's day has been the introduction of the modern motor cruiser in a style quite unlike the traditional Broads craft. These chromium-plated plastic bath-tubs not only look completely out of place, but tests have shown that they produce a higher bow wave than the traditional wooden hulls and inevitably cause more bank erosion. The worst culprits though are the day-boats, which were surely designed for more open water.

After World War 2, the numbers of hire craft rose steadily until around 1980. Since then, there has been a slow decline, which has been more than compensated for by the increase in numbers of private craft. It is still possible to hire traditional wooden craft from a few yards. The Norfolk County Sailing Base at Hunters Yard, Ludham, was operated by Norfolk County Council until 1995. There was a public outcry, in which the name Ransome figured prominently, when the Education Committee announced that it had decided to sell the yard and the unique fleet of yachts. The *Eastern Daily Press* gave their support to a scheme to buy the yard, and around £100,000 was donated by the public. The future of the enterprise was ensured by a grant from the Heritage Lottery Fund of £200,000.

Today, the Norfolk Heritage Fleet Trust operates the 13 beautiful mahog-any cabin yachts, which still retain their original oil lamps. The only concession to the twenty-first century has been the installation of bottled gas to replace the primus stoves. Sailing one of these lovely old cruisers on Barton Broad a year or so ago was an unforgettable experience for me, and the nearest thing to sailing the *Teasel* herself that anyone can have.

Albion, run by the Norfolk Wherry Trust, still sails, but she is of carvel construction instead of the much more usual clinker construction. At one time there were more than 200 trading wherries on the Broads. They were general carriers taking cargoes to all the riverside villages, each of which had its staithe. Most wherries were around 50 feet in length, car-

1969: **Albion** *rounds the bend by the Swan Inn, dwarfing a 14-foot dinghy*

And just then they heard the splash of a quant, and looked up the river. A wherry … was coming into sight around the bend. They knew the wherry, Sir Garnet, and they knew the skipper, Jim Woodall.

COOT CLUB

rying up to 40 tons of cargo. The 40-foot mast was carefully balanced so that lowering it to go under bridges really was as easy a business as Jim Woodall and Simon found it in *Sir Garnet*. *Albion* was built in 1898, and in the 1985 BBC film of *Coot Club* and *The Big Six* she did excellent duty as *Sir Garnet*, but there never was a wherry of that name, which came from a military boyhood hero of Ransome's. *Sir Garnet* was probably modelled on the wherry *Lord Roberts* that Ransome had moored alongside at Horning in 1934. There, was, however, a wherry called *Garnet*, which was built in Beccles about 150 years ago, but I do not know if she was still trading in Ransome's time. Today, the other surviving wherry is *Maud*, a long-term restoration project which should soon be sailing again. The pleasure wherries *Hathor* and *Solace* have been available for charter for some years. *Hathor* can carry a party of 12 and is operated by Peter Bower and Barny Matthews of Wroxham who also charter two wherry yachts of similar vintage.

The wherry **Albion** *and the old granary by the bridge at Wroxham, 1965*

Tom … ate his sandwiches his mother had given him for his dinner while sitting on the cabin roof of a business wherry, Sir Garnet, and talking to … her skipper.

COOT CLUB

The Norfolk Naturalists Trust is carrying on the good work of the Coot Club's Bird Protection Society. They have their Broadland Conservation Centre at Ranworth and a National Nature Reserve at Hickling Broad. At Hickling there is a water trail, and they have constructed some bird hides and a 60-foot observation tower. The bittern has declined in numbers and there are now only a handful of breeding pairs. The marsh harrier continues to breed at Hickling from time to time, but their records show only 23 pairs of bearded tits nested there in 1987. Coots, great-crested grebes, swans, herons and mallard are plentiful.

Mr Farland would feel very much at home in Horning today. A fleet of ten or so White Boats (as the Yare and Bure One Designs are known) sail and race regularly at Horning Sailing Club, just as they did in the 1930s. The class is still very popular, numbering 111. Of these, around 100 are still on the racing register, including three of the original craft built in 1908. In 1938, four years after the

At the staithe

appearance of *Coot Club,* one of the class was named *Grizzled Skipper,* which was the name of the yacht beaten by *Flash* by a bowsprit length at the end of the book. Recent hulls have been built of glass-fibre, but as all the boats are painted white, they look fine. I sailed as the guest of Horning Sailing Club on a blustery afternoon a year or so ago, and had an

Horning Staithe, 1990

Everyone knows the staithe, where the boats tie up when calling at Horning. Everyone knows the inn at the bend of the river above it ...

37

... and the boatbuilders' sheds below it.

Banham's boatyard, the model for Jonnatt's yard with its 'dentist's window'. It has now been replaced by some fine riverside houses.

exhilarating sail up the reach above the sailing club with water lapping the lee-rail in the gusts. There is nothing sedate about these Edwardian ladies!

Horning is the centre of the world of the Broadland stories. It is true that the Coots sail to Beccles and Potter Heigham, but they are, as Dorothea would put it, travellers to foreign parts. Fortunately, although there have been changes, the riverside village of Horning is just as delightful and friendly a place as it was 70 years ago. In the centre of the village, the staithe itself is almost unchanged. In fact, if you ignore the cars which seem as plentiful as boats, the tap which has replaced the pump on the green is almost the only evidence of progress. How fortunate it was that when the malthouses were pulled down in the 1920s, the parish decided to have the space beside the staithe kept as a grassed area!

Just above the staithe, the Swan Inn is not quite what it once was, having been extended and altered several times. Sadly, Edward Gillard's

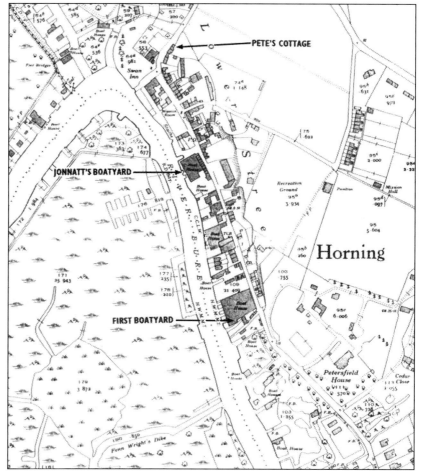

Ordnance Survey map of Horning, 1938

pike referred to in *The Big Six* no longer hangs in the bar. Following complaints from some diners it was removed and is now to be found in the Museum of the Broads at Stalham. The inn remains the focal point for local yachtsmen, who look in for their midday pints just as the boatbuilder fathers of the Coots did in *The Big Six*.

Below the staithe Banham's Boatyard, with its dentist's window overlooking the river that was the model for Jonnatt's yard, has been replaced

Pete's cottage, 1972

'Think they'll drag the river?' said Joe. But Bill did not answer and they ran grimly on, round the corner by the inn, and so to the row of cottages, one of which was Pete's home.

THE BIG SIX

by some fine riverside houses. Over the years I have seen two or three converted lifeboats, looking very much like mastless *Death and Glories*, in Horning Reach. It would be fascinating to know if Ransome saw one of them when he was staying at White Gates while he was at work on *The Big Six*.

Across from the staithe in the village street, Roy's Stores, where the

Death and Glories had money to burn, is under different ownership these days. The shop is the one which looks as though it was built in the front garden of a thatched cottage near the Swan Inn.

A short way down the road towards the ferry is White Gates, now a private house. Any one of the original cottages nearby would do for Mr Tedder's cottage, but Pete's cottage, just around the corner from the Swan, was pulled down some years ago to be replaced by a more modern cottage. A few hundred yards down the road to the ferry is the large boatshed where Tom and Joe saw the flash of the villain's torch. Beyond the yard, the road curves out of sight of the shops and the scene can have changed little in the last 60 years. The willow pattern harbour is still recognisable, but explorers will look in vain for Dr Dudgeon's house among the dykes and willows on the right-hand side. The location of the Coot Club dyke was probably just beyond the old Chumley and Hawkes boatyard which was built there in the 1920s. Nowadays,

Dr Dudgeon listened carefully. Presently he stepped over the fence. The others scrambled over and took him through the bushes to the Death and Glory.

THE BIG SIX

The Wilderness, 1999. The wind-pump is now a holiday cottage.

Bungalows have been built on what was once the Wilderness, a marshy bit of land with an old wind-pump on it.

THE BIG SIX

the area is devoted to waterside holiday cottages.

In *The Big Six* Ransome mentions the changes between the time of the story (1932) and the time of writing (1940), that occurred to the river bank on what had been the Wilderness. Since then the number of bungalows has considerably increased, the dyke has been widened and the area has been fully developed. The Wilderness did exist and can be identified on old maps of the area, and the stretch of marshy ground is still remembered by local folk who played there in their youth.

41

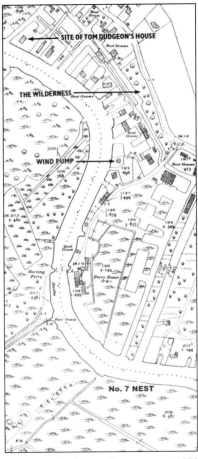

SITE OF TOM DUDGEON'S HOUSE

THE WILDERNESS

WIND PUMP

No. 7 NEST

Ordnance Survey map, 1938

Great changes have taken place in the area of the Ferry Inn. What amounts to the commercial part of the village has moved from one end to the other and now includes a marina as well as several boatyards. The present Ferry Inn is not the building in which Bill's aunt worked, as this was bombed on 26th April 1941. Four bombs struck the inn and another fell on the ferry pontoon. At the time, the bar was crowded and 21 lives

As he shot past the Ferry, he saw George Owdon leaning on the white-painted rail of the ferry-raft and looking down at him.

COOT CLUB

The Ferry Inn, 1934

RY HOTEL
USE

were lost and several people seriously injured. The inn was rebuilt, but that building did not last long and was destroyed by fire. The present building occupies a site dating from the eleventh century.

In recent years, a foot ferry has operated from the site of the former ferry to take fishermen to the further bank and visitors to the walkway to Cockshoot Broad. Below the ferry, the ditch where the villains fell after Bill had removed the plank was widened years ago and now leads to the marina. It was much quieter when I first moored there in 1956. One morning I looked out of the cabin windows straight into the eyes of a bittern standing on the bank not a yard away. I was so amazed that I forgot all about taking a photograph and just watched it walk away.

There is now no sign of the eelman's old sett by Black Horse Broad, but Horning still has its eelmen who live in houses and not in hulks and whose nets are often seen hanging up

Eel fisher's hut on the Bure

to dry on their boats moored by the New Inn. Their modern Fyke nets are not only more efficient, but can be set up where the eel fisher chooses at different states of the tide.

Tom Cable, who was fishing for eels at Kendal or Candle Dyke in the 1930s, recalls that he used to fish for a period of five nights when the moon was on the wane. Wet and windy nights when it was particularly

dark were considered the best conditions. He fished for mature silver eels. 'Stream' eels reach maturity at about ten years, when they turn from yellow to silver underneath. He reckoned that male eels were two to the pound and female eels weighed from a pound and a half to six pounds. The net was expensive and when it was raised a red light was displayed and during the day notices warned crews

of passing vessels not to quant. The net was always raised when the ride was ebbing and was kept in place for five hours. It was lowered after the first of the flood had washed the rubbish back out of the nets.

Almost five miles upstream from Horning are the twin villages of

Ranworth Broad, 1972

Wroxham and Hoveton. Trains from Norwich still stop at the station, and in the village itself the store where Mrs Barrable bought the D's cheap oilskins has developed out of all recognition. The old bridge remains, but the granary which stood beside it has been replaced by the Riverside Centre. A small boatyard was opened in Wroxham well over 100 years ago, and it has been suggested that the boat-letting industry started here. Even today, Wroxham is one of the most important centres on the Broads, and it is still vibrant with activity similar to that which impressed Dick and Dorothea when they arrived. The strongest image, however, is of a con-

'It's the most gorgeous lake,' said Dorothea. 'We've rowed all round it. It's full of good hiding places.'

COOT CLUB

stant stream of cars crossing the bridge throughout the season.

Downstream from Horning, the river meanders past several places where the coot with the white feather could very well have nested, until the narrow dyke leading to Ranworth is reached. Ransome called the broad Ranworth Broad, but today visitors know it as Malthouse Broad. Ranworth is a popular port of call and there are usually 20 or so motor cruisers moored stern-on to the staithe. The Maltsters public house stands at the road junction and looks across to the staithe where the old granary has been replaced by a useful store and an information centre. Nearby there is a children's play area and a nature trail leading to the nature reserve of Ranworth Broad and its conservation centre. A little way up the hill is the post office where Dick and Dorothea sent picture postcards home. It is all very pleasant, but Ranworth today is no longer the quiet backwater where Tom lay low and the Death and Glories tried to emigrate from their troubles.

`We'll never get through it, will we?' said Dick, who was again at the tiller, 'even with the mast right down?'

COOT CLUB

Explorers should not miss the River Ant just because it hardly features in the books. It is very much Ransome country with its reed fringed banks and meadowland. A five miles per hour speed limit operates throughout its length and perhaps this helps to keep it noticeably quieter than the River Bure. At How Hill there is an environmental and field study centre devoted to the traditional Broadland way of life and the wildlife of the area. In this part of the Broads, the

Hoping to catch another whopper? Fishing close to the place where the World's Whopper was caught on the River Thurne, 1999.

Old Bob says 'Come along': 'Old Barbar' with his motor tug **Surprise** *towing the Ransomes' Fairway through the Yarmouth bridges in 1933*

and if there is room they can moor in the dyke by the windmill, just as *Teasel* did.

Voyagers to the southern waters pass through one bridge fewer in Yarmouth these days. Anyone in trouble can still contact the Yacht Station who can call on reliable watermen like the owner of the *Come Along*. The *Come Along* was based on a real craft operated by 'Old Barbar' who towed Ransome through the

swallowtail butterfly can still be seen and at night the occasional booming of the bittern is heard.

The River Thurne will seem familiar to Ransome readers. Potter Heigham bridge still provides its age-old challenge to helmsmen, and a short way upstream, where the former railway bridge used to cross, a new road bridge keeps through traffic away from the old bridge. Above Potter Heigham bridge, the twenty-first-century explorer can still enter the world of the Coot Club. Readers can follow the path along the rond and try to decide just where the world's whopper was caught, and at Martham they will find a boatyard still hiring traditional wooden boats. The river continues upstream for several miles and the whole area remains unspoilt. Hickling Broad and Horsey Mere await the sailor, who can try quanting through the dyke where Dick fell in

Yarmouth bridges on more than one occasion. Across the entrance to Breydon Water, the railway bridge has been replaced by a modern road bridge, but beyond the bridge the great expanse of Breydon Water with its two lines of posts marking the deepwater channel has not changed. At the far end of the channel, the Berney Arms still stands in splendid isolation, but boats passing along the New Cut will find that there is no need for anyone to hold out the butterfly net to collect tolls for passing under the lifting road bridge. Oulton Broad remains a very popular stretch of water but it looks very little like the photographs that the Ransomes took on their visits.

Beccles, however, is still a very pleasant town. The malthouses beside the staithe have largely gone, but the road leading up into the town was as empty as in Ransome's drawing when I walked up it one Sunday morning recently. On the right-hand side, narrow passages called scores lead down to the river just as they did in *Coot Club*. The road itself heads up

towards the church where the old wall still looks out over the river. In *Coot Club*, the *Teasel* moored at the public staithe and the *Welcome of Rochester* was moored on the other side of the river by Beccles Mill which has long since gone. *Welcome* was based on a real barge, the *Pudge*, which Ransome moored alongside when he called at Beccles. *Pudge* is still afloat and available for charter parties.

Romance came to life again as, after a last look at the Teasel and the distant barge, they left the staithe and walked up the long street into the town.

COOT CLUB

Tom came out again with the map and glanced at the long line of red posts on the port side, and the long line of black posts on the starboard side, leading away into the distance.

COOT CLUB

◀ *Breydon Water, 1999*

Beccles Mill, 1999. Only the tall chimney remains. ▶

Port and Starboard, bursting with pride, pointed across the river at the Welcome of Rochester moored by the mill.

COOT CLUB

In the wake of *Goblin*, *Wizard* and *Firefly*

Pin Mill has changed very little since *Nancy Blackett* and *Lapwing* lay at their moorings in the river. The essential car park is small and unobtrusive, and the picnic area has been pleasantly set out. The waterfront itself still looks very like the illustrations Ransome drew so carefully in 1938. The sixteenth-century Butt and Oyster provides splendid 'breakfasts' for today's Jim Bradings, and the interior appears much as it did in the days when it was the haunt of working sailormen. Sitting in the old bow window of the bar as the high tide laps the wall a few feet below is an experience Ransome admirers will long remember. Nearby, the three adjoining cottages, Alma Cottage, Riverside Cottage and Seagulls, were formerly the Alma Inn. This was sold

by Cobbolds, the Ipswich brewers, in 1910. It was bought by Annie Powell in 1918 and she lived there until

her death in the 1950s. It is almost certain that, in the days when Ransome was writing, the present proper-

The Butt and Oyster and Alma Cottage as drawn by Arthur Ransome

ties were still one and Annie Powell was living with her unmarried brother Jack. He made the sails for the Thames barges in the sail loft next door, in the building which is now the yacht chandlers. After Powell's marriage he and his wife occupied the part which is now Seagulls. Alma was for many years kept as a holiday cottage, but at Riverside Cottage next door, climbing roses still cling to the wall where the windows look out on a scene where land, in comparison to water, still seems hardly to matter at all. Hetty Watts, who has the good fortune to look out through those windows, told me she often hears cries of 'There's Alma Cottage!' from the lane outside. The hard in front of the Butt goes out a long way at low water but dinghies use the stream, which runs beside it, just as *Wizard* does in *Secret Water*. The stream, or Grindle as it is called, silts up and has to be cleared out by hand each year.

Harry King's boatyard no longer builds wooden boats, but they seem to have plenty of repair work and fitting out to do. The yard is still in the family, being run by Harry's grandson Geoff. Some years ago, Harry King's son Sam told me that he remembered *Selina King* and *Peter Duck* being built, and in 1938 he built Ransome's second *Swallow* dinghy. I had particular interest in the boat, as it had recently come into my possession and I wanted to try to restore it. It was right and proper that after her

The same scene at Pin Mill photographed in 1999

. . . this happy place where almost everybody wore sea-boots, and land, in comparison with water, seemed hardly to matter at all.

WE DIDN'T MEAN TO GO TO SEA

51

successful restoration *Swallow* should be relaunched at Pin Mill in 1992, but sadly, by then Sam King had died. Ransome spent much time at the yard during the building of *Selina King,* and he planned to write a book about her building. Evgenia chose the name *Selina* and when Harry King heard, he told Ransome that he had an aunt of that name. 'Then we shall call her *Selina King,*' replied Ransome. Sam also built Ransome a tiny dinghy, the *Queen Mary,* as a tender to *Nancy.* In those days dinghies were built by eye, without plans, using just a couple of moulds which were removed after the timbers were fastened. With the outbreak of war, Harry King set aside some timber for Ransome and Major Busk to build yachts when peace returned. This explains how it was that *Peter Duck* could be built so soon after hostilities had ceased when timber was in very short supply.

Peter Duck is in very good shape after some extensive restoration, following her years in Russian waters. *Nancy Blackett* was at Scarborough for a number of years and became neglected.and damaged by a car which fell on her from the quay where she was moored. By one of those strange coincidences, she was bought and saved from an ignominious fate by Michael Rines who lives not much more than an arrow's flight from the Ransomes' old home at Broke Farm. *Nancy* now belongs to a charitable trust set up by some members of the Arthur Ransome Society and, having been returned to her former glory, is now officially recognised as a 'historic vessel'.

Selina King, after Ransome had sold the vessel, spent some years based on the South Coast, before crossing the Atlantic to Bermuda where Hal White used her for a number of years as a charter yacht for Caribbean cruises. After White parted with *Selina King,* she spent a period sailing off Florida, before he discovered the vessel in a run-down state. Somehow he managed to acquire and restore *Selina King,* and in 1999 she returned to Bermudan waters under his command.

The Orwell with its wooded banks is still a beautiful river. Many more people use the Orwell these days since the opening of the marinas at Levington, Woolverstone and Shotley. Helmsmen in the river are no longer distracted by the sight of porpoises bobbing up, perhaps due to pollution and increased traffic. Down river, the Felixstowe bank has altered beyond recognition. The old part has been swallowed up by the huge container port. More than two miles of container termini are served by container transit areas upwards of half a mile in depth. In the midst of this, the old Felixstowe Dock is almost hidden. It used to be at the end of a public road which led to the mills, bus terminus, sheds, the Pier Hotel and a few houses. Now the approach to the ferry is down a heavily caged-in footpath through the dock complex. Beside the old dock, some of the mills seen from the *Goblin* still stand, but the Pier Hotel is no more. The rank commercialism of the port and the sheer functional lines of the ships have stripped the place of all romance. Ransome would hate it.

Downstream the old Landguard

Pin Mill hard and the River Orwell, 1999: Tony Ward, the Pin Mill harbour master, comes ashore after making a round of the mooring buoys.

fort, which has stood guarding the harbour mouth since the seventeenth century, is unchanged. Off Landguard Point is the Beach End buoy. The buoy no longer has the wave-actuated bell that confused the crew of the *Goblin*. This was shifted to its neigh-bour, the North-west Beach buoy, when massive dredging operations eased the right-angle bend into the harbour, around which the huge con-tainer vessels were unable to navigate. The buoy has also changed colour since the internationally agreed buoy-age system came into operation in 1977 when it was painted green. The sound of the Cork lightship's beu...eueueueueu no longer warns mariners in the harbour of mist along the coast as the lightship was removed some years ago, and the area is now marked by lighted buoys.

Across the water Harwich has fared better. The town has become a happy blend of old and new and its skyline is little changed. It is still dominated by the spire of St Nicholas Church, and on the Quay, opposite Ha'penny Pier, the old Town Hall into which Jim Brading hurried to find the har-bour master for news of his missing ship, has been redeveloped. The har-bour master now has his own building topped by aerials and radar scanners on the river's edge which houses the Port Control Station. It is all so much more organised these days.

Shotley still has its wooden piers, but there is no longer any employ-ment for Lieutenant-Commanders, as HMS *Ganges* closed some years ago. The new marina has brought life back to that side of the river and some

Bridget Island (right), Swallow Island in the distance and (left) Mastodon Island, 1988

The rest of the secret archipelago is delightfully quiet and peaceful. Quiet, that is, except for the constant chatter of the gulls. In *Secret Water* Ransome, who was so careful with technical details and who delighted in solving technical problems, avoided all reference to spring or neap tides. Channels which are navigable by dinghies on spring tides are impassable at other times. On this part of the east coast, the spring tides occur when high water is about 2 pm, yet *Wizard* and *Firefly* made their passages when high water was at nine o'clock in the morning. The scene that Ransome describes, with the water right up to the saltings, occurs with spring tides. Martin Lewis spent many holidays exploring and he sent me his fascinating illustrated logs. He navigated the North-west Passage and felt it might still be possible to do the North-east Passage on a high spring tide, although he never succeeded. The Cruising Association prewar chart of the area is very much like Ransome's map. The present-day charts look as if there has been more

new housing and a sports complex have replaced the naval establishment. Up the river a couple of sad redundant lightships rot quietly at their moorings. For all the changes the container port has brought about, Orwell Haven is still a glorious and sheltered stretch of water, which becomes full of little ships on summer weekends when yachts come down from Pin Mill and the marinas. A little careful navigation will bring seaborne explorers to the entrance of Secret Water. Away to port, Amazon Creek opens up, and at high water it is quite a highway leading towards moorings near Walton and the Tichmarsh Marina around Cape Horn.

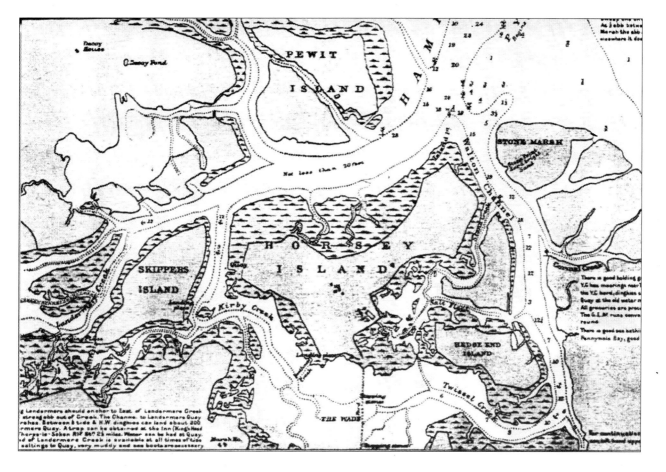

Royal Cruising Club 1913 chart of Secret Water

> 'You can get right up to the town at high water in a dinghy. But if you do, don't wait there too long, or there won't be water to take you back.'
>
> SECRET WATER

The head of Amazon Creek, 1973 ▶

◀ *Red Sea at low water, 1998*

> 'Why is your totem an eel?' said Titty. 'Mud everywhere,' said the Mastodon. 'Eels like it and so do we.'
>
> SECRET WATER

erosion along the north shore of Secret Water, and Blackberry Coast has effectively disappeared. One or two yachts still anchor off Flint Island just as *Lapwing* did, but *Goblin*'s (and *Nancy Blackett*'s) old anchorage off Swallow Island is now unusable because of the oyster beds. However, in the channel between Bridget Island, Mastodon Island and the mainland there are several delightful moorings. Explorers on land can leave their car in a park near the Naze tower and walk along the cliffs and beside a nature reserve until Amazon Creek is reached. Flint Island's sandy shore is visible to the north, and in the other direction the sea wall leads up the creek towards Walton. Walton-on-the-Naze itself is a pleasant, small seaside town which seems as though it has not changed too much through the years. The Eels' instructions for finding the boatbuilders can be followed

Long years ago there must have been busy barge traffic in and out from this old quay when there were no railways and poor roads and everything that could be was carried by water.

SECRET WATER

Witch's Quay, 1975

without trouble, and near to the boat-builders is the head of Amazon Creek. Leaving Walton, little over a mile down the road towards Kirby Le Soken, a lane beside a farm leads to the Red Sea. As the Red Sea is reached, the path rises over the sea wall to come to a stop at an inland sea at high tide. At low water, the road leads temptingly towards Swallow Island. It is just as Ransome described it; a firm gravel base covered by puddles and a layer of soft mud. The four posts in the middle have gone, although several withies mark the way. On one visit, I followed a smartly dressed rider as her horse splashed across to the island and I spotted some bait diggings like those which puzzled Titty and Bridget. The causeway seems to be well used, for one Ransome enthusiast told me that when he went across to explore Swallow Island he had to wait for a furniture van to cross!

A footpath along the sea wall leads from the Wade towards Witch's Quay.

I have visited Witch's Quay several times and every time I have been aware of a strong sense of timelessness. It is as if the world has forgotten the old barge quay and its former granary. Civilisation seems to be miles away, although it is lurking just out of sight down the lane to the south. The witch's cottage is in good repair and has been in use as a holiday cottage for a number of years. The owners were presented with a beautifully carved eel totem by a grateful enthusiast. Some years ago, the cottage was used as the base for the Malachite film *A Voyage with Nancy Blackett*. We managed to launch *Swallow II* there, and I made my contribution to the film aboard the dinghy. The old granary itself has been renovated and is once more a home with a very special view, and at the north end of the lane is another house with a glorious outlook across the saltings to Swallow Island.

The marks which were so confusing to the young map makers must have been spotted by Ransome somewhere or other, but they are no good for marking creeks which dry out

Crossing the Wade

at half tide and below. If the line from the buoy to the mooring is long enough to allow them to float at high water, they float further and further from the channel they are supposed to mark, as the tide goes out, and are no longer accurate enough. Withies are the only answer. Mastodon Island is now a nature reserve, and the warden has replaced the Mastodon as the island's only inhabitant. Like Swal-

low Island, it is linked to the mainland by a causeway.

The area south west of Mastodon Island is much more interesting than the Secret Archipelago Expedition's map suggests. Martin Lewis carried on where they left off and has mapped it most carefully. Two or three Thames barges have rotted away in Secret Water. Gillian Beevor (née Busk) could not remember *Speedy* from her

The Wade, 1998

The road was much better than they had thought. There were deep puddles in it left by the tide. There was a layer of soft mud over it, but never deep enough to cover their ankles. Under the mud there was good hard gravel, and it was easy walking, though they found it best not to walk too near together, because nobody could help splashing the mud about.

SECRET WATER

map-making trip, but Jim Clay told Christina Hardyment that there was once a barge which had one end turned into a cabin.

From Witch's Quay it is possible to follow the sea wall north until Goblin Creek is reached. Here, overlooking Ransome's favourite anchorage, is a good place to conclude our tour of the places that he immortalised in

The shores were widening on either side, and they were coming out in a broad lake of shimmering water which covered the sea of mud that they had seen in the morning. Here and there, ahead of them, a withy waved gently in the tide.

SECRET WATER

Red Sea at High Water, 1988

the four books set in East Anglia, for it has changed so little since Ransome first brought up here in *Nancy Blackett* in September 1936 when he wrote in his log:

Rouse [his crew] *this time suggested anchoring, and having tea, which we did at 5 pm (in Hamford Water). Later when the ebb slackened, we moved into Kirby Creek with the last of the daylight, and shared a very nice quiet anchorage with a single persistent curlew.*

61

Bibliography

The two main sources of Ransome material are to be found in the Brotherton Collection at the University of Leeds and the Ransome Collection at the Abbot Hall Museum, Kendal.

Altounyan, Taqui. *In Aleppo Once.* John Murray, 1969

Beesley, Julia. *What to Do On the Norfolk Broads.* Jarrold, 1988

Broads Authority. *Broads Plan.* 1987

Broads Authority. *Ranworth Staithe Case Study.* 1983

◀ *Filming at the witch's cottage, 1993: the author aboard Arthur Ransome's* **Swallow II** *dinghy being interviewed by Charles Maplestone for the Malachite television film* **A Voyage with Nancy Blackett**

Brogan, Hugh. *The Life of Arthur Ransome.* Jonathan Cape, 1984

Coote, Jack. *East Coast Rivers from the Air.* Yachting Monthly

Hardyment, Christina. *Arthur Ransome and Captain Flint's Trunk.* Jonathan Cape, 1984

Hay, David and Joan. *East Anglia from the Sea.* Stanford, 1972

Ransome, Arthur. *Peter Duck.* Jonathan Cape, 1932

Ransome, Arthur. *Coot Club.* Jonathan Cape, 1934

Ransome, Arthur. *We Didn't Mean to Go to Sea.* Jonathan Cape, 1937

Ransome, Arthur. *Secret Water.* Jonathan Cape, 1939

Ransome, Arthur. *The Big Six.* Jonathan Cape, 1940

Ransome, Arthur. *Autobiography,* ed. by Rupert Hart-Davis. Jonathan Cape, 1976

Ransome, Arthur. *Coots in the North and Other Stories,* ed. by Hugh Brogan. Jonathan Cape, 1988

Ransome, Arthur. *Signalling from Mars: The Letters of Arthur Ransome,* ed. by Hugh Brogan. Jonathan Cape, 1997

Stephens, George. *100 Pictures of the Norfolk Broads.* Jarrold, 1927

Wardale, Roger. *Nancy Blackett: Under Sail with Arthur Ransome.* Jonathan Cape, 1991

Wardale, Roger. *Arthur Ransome and the World of the Swallows and Amazons.* Great Northern, 2000